This journal belongs to:

The Leadership
Journal

Welcome to this powerful journal! This journal was inspired by the anthology *Experts & Influencers: Leadership Edition.* (A great companion book to read while capturing your insights, wisdom, and ideas in this powerful journal.) Our desire in creating this journal is to provide you with a tool to support you on your leadership journey of discovering your leadership gifts and leadership style, and building your leadership tool box. This journal is designed to help you listen to your leadership wisdom, insights, and heart so that you can fully claim your leadership and share the gift of you in all of your brilliance and share it with the world. To lead with confidence, compassion, wisdom, joy...using all of your leadership talents and gifts powerfully to lead, lift others up, serve powerfully, and SHINE!

In these pages you'll find room to explore and capture your thoughts, reflections, and ideas, as well as hear the messages your heart and spirit are wanting to share with you. At the outside corner of each page you will see a bird-in-flight graphic to remind you that we get to soar together, and as Henry Ford says: *"When everything seems to be going against you, remember that the airplane takes off against the wind, not with it."*

I encourage you to take some time each day to stop, pause, and listen to what is being spoken into your heart and spirt and give yourself the opportunity to bring this powerful information and insight forward by writing it out. We left you lots of open lines and room to capture your thoughts and insights.

For those of you who like to have something to respond to or write about...we also wanted to give you some possible reflection points and tips to support you.

1. **We would encourage you to get a copy of the *Experts & Influencers: Leadership Edition* anthology, compiled by Rebecca Hall Gruyter.** (This powerful book has great tips and deep, powerful shares by multiple experts coming together to empower you to fully step into your leadership calling. Every chapter gives you powerful steps and insights you can take in your life.)

2. **We encourage you to reflect on the following Reflection Points:**

   a. What leadership gift, skill, activity, or way of being are you discovering about yourself?

   b. How can you use this leadership discovery about you to step or move forward in areas of your life that are most important to you?

   c. Where are you feeling blocked? And how can you possibly move through or around the block?

   d. What areas in life are most important to you?

   e. How can you share more of you and your unique leadership gifting with more people?

   f. Where have you been hiding some of your leadership gifts?

   g. How can you bring more of your gifts forward?

   h. What three things are you celebrating doing, being, seeing, and/or receiving today?

3. **Tap into another part of you activity.** Write a question with your dominant hand (the hand you normally use to write). Then put your pen/pencil in your other hand (your non-dominant hand) and write a response/answer to the question. This taps into the opposite side of the brain from where you normally go for answers and information when writing. You will find great insight and wisdom by accessing more of you, especially parts of your mind you aren't always going to for information and insights. Remember, handwriting doesn't count...feel in and receive this powerful information and insight by tapping into more of you....and listening and receiving.

4. **Listen to music that helps you pause, reflect and be present to your thoughts and take.** Take several breaths to center yourself —perhaps light a candle to represent lighting your brilliance and sharing with the world. Then, take 5-10 minutes to write what comes to your heart and spirit...not analyzing, just writing and seeing what your heart and spirit have to say to you today.

5. **Remember, you are a gift and absolutely needed in this world.** Here are some additional reflection points for you to consider on those days you are looking for some writing prompts to get you started. Be willing to take time to celebrate the gift of you, of life, and be willing to share the gift of you with others. In light of this, write a response to the following questions:

    a. What is your leadership thought for the day?

    b. What is your leadership action for today?

    c. What is your leadership discovery for today?

    d. What insight/idea/suggestion/reminder are you being given about your leadership journey?

    e. What leadership experience are you celebrating today?

The next step is yours.

Remember…

> *"It only takes one person to make you happy and change your life: YOU."*

> ~Charles Orlando

> *"The most effective way to do it, is to do it."*

> ~Amelia Earhart

> *"You were designed for accomplishment, engineered for success, and endowed with the seeds of greatness!"*

> ~Zig Ziglar

Drink in the insights and wisdom that support and inspire you. Take the time to pause, read, and reflect. Listen to the powerful messages of hope that are waiting for you within these transformational and dynamic pages. It's not an accident that you purchased or were given this journal and are opening it to read and write. I invite you to lean in and truly receive the messages and wisdom that will speak to your heart and soul. We can't wait to see you STEP INTO YOUR LEADERSHIP GIFTS FULLY AND LOOK FORWARD TO SEEING YOU SHINE!

-----*Rebecca Hall Gruyter, Book Compiler*

Founder/Owner of Your Purpose Driven Practice and CEO of RHG Media Productions

Closing Thoughts

I hope you have been touched by this journal and it has provided you a powerful time of connection and reflection. Listed below, please find tools, books (available on Amazon) and resources that can further support you on stepping further and further into your brilliance and sharing it out powerfully. As we believe what the world needs is more of YOU. We can't wait to see you, hear from you, and celebrate you as you share the gift of you with the world! May you always choose to *live on purpose and with great purpose...and SHINE in your leadership and brilliance!*

****

Books compiled or written by Rebecca Hall Gruyter to be released in 2019 and 2020:

The Animal Legacies!

This anthology features authors sharing heart-warming, inspiring, and empowering true stories of how animals have forever touched their lives. They will share profound lessons they learned, powerful truths, encouraging messages, and a celebration and honor of their animal friends. Every reader will be encouraged, his heart touched, as each writer shares and passes on his own animal legacy. We know this book will touch your heart and your life in beautiful, empowering ways. (To be released December 2019).

The Expert and Influencers Series: Women's Empowerment Edition

This powerful anthology will feature up to 30 experts and influencers committed to inform and uplift you in the area of Women's Empowerment. From their personal and professional leadership experiences, each author will share tips, advice, and powerful insights to help you step forward as a leader in your life and business. (To be released June 2020).

Step Into Your Mission and Purpose!

This book, the second in our *Step Into* anthology series, takes the reader through the next step in his journey to SHINE! Featuring up to 30 authors, this anthology empowers readers to embrace their brilliance and choice to discover their unique mission and purpose in life. You will learn what it means to make the choice to live your life on purpose and with purpose. Each chapter, through the wisdom of this selection of authors, will empower and equip you to develop your own practice of living your purpose every day. Because the world needs you and your brilliance! (To be released 2021).

Anthologies Available Now That Are Compiled by Rebecca Hall Gruyter:

SHINE Series (Compiled and led by Rebecca Hall Gruyter)

Come out of Hiding and SHINE! (Book 1 in the SHINE Series)

Bloom Where You are Planted and SHINE! (Book 2 in the SHINE Series)

Step Forward and SHINE! (Book 3 and final book in the SHINE Series)

Step Into Series (Compiled and led by Rebecca Hall Gruyter)

Step Into Your Brilliance! (2019, Book 1 in the Step Into Series)

Step Into Your Mission & Purpose! (2021, Book 2 in the Step Into Series)

Experts & Influencers Series (Compiled and led by Rebecca Hall Gruyter)

Experts & Influencers Series: Leadership (2019, Book 1 in the Series)

Experts & Influencers Series: Women's Empowerment (2020, Book 2 in the Series)

The Grandmother Legacies (Anthology Compiled by Rebecca Hall Gruyter)

Empowering YOU, Transforming Lives (365 Daily Inspiration Anthology Compiled by Rebecca Hall Gruyter)

Books Available Now Featuring a Chapter by Rebecca Hall Gruyter:

The 40/40 Rules Anthology compiled by Holly Porter

Becoming Outrageously Successful Anthology compiled by Dr. Anita Jackson

Catch Your Star Anthology published by THRIVE Publishing

Discover Your Destiny Anthology compiled by Denise Joy Thompson

I Am Beautiful Anthology compiled by Teresa Hawley-Howard

The Power of Our Voices, Sharing Our Story Anthology compiled by Teresa Hawley-Howard

Succeeding Against All Odds Anthology compiled by Sandra Yancey

Success Secrets for Today's Feminine Entrepreneurs Anthology compiled by Dr. Anita Jackson

Unstoppable Woman of Purpose Anthology and workbook, compiled by Nella Chikwe

Women on a Mission Anthology compiled by Teresa Hawley-Howard

Women of Courage, Women of Destiny Anthology compiled by Dr. Anita Jackson

Women Warriors Who Make It Rock Anthology compiled by Nichole Peters

You Are Whole, Perfect, and Complete - Just As You Are Anthology compiled by Carol Plummer and Susan Driscoll

Dear Powerful Reader,

Thank you for reading our journal. I hope it has encouraged and empowered and uplifted you.

I wanted to share a little bit more about our organizations, Your Purpose Driven Practice™, RHG TV Network™, RHG Publishing™ and RHG Media Productions™. We are passionate about helping others live on purpose and with purpose in their life and business. I hope this book has supported and inspired you to choose to live on purpose and with great purpose in your leadership!

If you are wanting to reach more people and be part of inspiring and supporting others with your message, your gifts, and the work that you bring to the world, then I want to share some opportunities for you to consider.

Each year we compile and produce anthology book projects, support authors in publishing their own powerful books as bestsellers, produce and publish an international magazine, launch TV shows, facilitate women's empowerment conferences, get quoted in major media, launch radio and podcast shows, help experts and speakers step into a place of powerful influence to make a global difference. We provide programs and strategies to help you reach more people and facilitate the Speaker Talent Search (which helps speakers, experts, and influencers connect with more speaking opportunities). We would love to support you in reaching more people. Please take a moment to learn a little bit more about us at the sites listed below, and then reach out to us for a conversation. **We would love to help you be Seen, Heard, Have Impact and SHINE!**

You can learn more about each of these things are our main website:
www.YourPurposeDrivenPractice.com

Enjoy our powerful **TV and podcast shows**:
www.RHGTVNetwork.com

Learn more about the **Speaker Talent Search™**:
www.SpeakerTalentSearch.com

Learn more about our **writing opportunities**:

http://yourpurposedrivenpractice.com/writing-opportunities/

If you would like to connect with me personally to explore some of our opportunities in upcoming book projects, podcast/radio shows, and/or TV, then here is the link to schedule a time to speak with me directly: www.MeetWithRebecca.com,

or you can email me at: Rebecca@YourPuposeDrivenPractice.com

May you always choose to Be Seen, Heard, Have Impact and SHINE!

Warmly,

Rebecca Hall Gruyter

Rebecca Hall Gruyter is an Influencer and Empowerment Leader committed to bringing Experts and Influencers forward so that together we can lean in and make the world a better place, one heart and life at a time. She is the owner of *Your Purpose Driven Practice*, creator of the *Women's Empowerment Series* events/TV show, the *Speaker Talent Search™*, and *Your Success Formula™*. Rebecca is an in-demand speaker, an expert money coach, and a frequent guest expert on success panels, tele-summits, TV, and radio shows. Rebecca specializes in using her over 10 million promotional reach to help you be seen, heard, and SHINE!

As the CEO of *RHG Media Productions™*, Rebecca launched the international TV Network (www.RHGTVNetwork.com) to bring even more positive and transformational programming to the world. In July 2017, she launched the Global RHG Magazine & TV Guide, bringing inspirational influences to the world and their messages! In January 2018, she expanded RHG Publishing to now help individual authors bring their books forward as bestsellers so they can be positioned as they bring their powerful book forward.

Rebecca is a popular and syndicated radio talk show host, #1 bestselling author (multiple times), and publisher who wants to help YOU impact the world powerfully!

(925) 787-1572

Rebecca@YourPurposeDrivenPractice.com

www.facebook.com/rhallgruyter (Facebook)

www.YourPurposeDrivenPractice.com (Main Website)

www.RHGTVNetwork.com (TV Network)

www.SpeakerTalentSearch.com (Free Opportunity for Speakers to get on More Stages)

www.EmpoweringWomenTransformingLives.com (Weekly Radio Show)

www.MeetWithRebecca.com (Calendar link to schedule a time to talk with Rebecca)

Made in the USA
Monee, IL
04 November 2020